T0105550

WHAT ABOUT YOUR SOUL?

by
Pastor Johnny James

Order this book online at www.trafford.com
or email orders@trafford.com

Most Trafford titles are also available at major online book retailers.

Printed in Victoria, BC, Canada.

ISBN: 978-1-4269-3321-9

*Our mission is to efficiently provide the world's finest, most comprehensive book publishing
service, enabling every author to experience success. To find out how to publish your book, your
way, and have it available worldwide, visit us online at www.trafford.com*

Trafford rev. 06/01/2010

www.trafford.com

North America & international
toll-free: 1 888 232 4444 (USA & Canada)
phone: 250 383 6864 ♦ fax: 812 355 4082

This book is dedicated to every soul on the face of this earth

Preface

This book brings to our attention the most important question that we will ever have to answer. This question is about the eternity of our soul. This book gives biblical illustrations of some people in the bible who were not concerned about this question until it was too late. So this book serves as a warning to those who do not know and a wake up call to those who do know about the eternity of the soul. The question that we need to answer now is where will our soul live eternally, with God or separated from God?

Table of Contents

CHAPTER ONE

What About Your Soul?

The most important question that we ask ourselves as we live out our lives in this world should not be how much material wealth we can accumulate in our lifetime. But the number one question that every human being on the face of this earth should be asking themselves is "What about my soul"? In other words, "If I died right now in this very hour, where will my soul spend eternity"? This is a personal question that each person must answer for themselves. God has already done his part when He sent His only begotten Son into this world to suffer many things at the hands of sinful men. On the cross, Jesus took our place. He gave his life as a dying sacrifice that we would accept Him and live the rest of our lives as a living sacrifice for Him. As we look into the word of God, we will find out where the soul was originated. Genesis 2:7, "And the Lord God formed man of the dust of the ground, and breathed into his nostrils the breath of life; And man became A LIVING SOUL". In this verse we see that God took almost nothing and made man. He did not even use a piece of dirt, but all God used was the dust of the ground. It was God who breathed into man's nostrils man's first breath of life. Just as we could not breath on our own in the beginning without God, we still cannot breath on our own without God helping us to breath. Even after man was formed of the dust of the ground, he was just lying there breathless until God gave him the first breath of life and man then became a living soul. Man's soul became just like God, Eternal. In other words our soul will never die. When our physical bodies have returned back to the dust of the ground from whence they came, our soul will live in eternity somewhere. Either with God or away from God, the choice is ours to make. So my question to you again is "WHAT ABOUT YOUR SOUL?"

Luke chapter 12:16-24, tells us about a man who went through life with the wrong priorities and because of this he forgot all about his soul, just as so many have also done today. Verse 16, "and He spake a parable unto them, saying the ground of a certain rich man brought forth plentifully". This man failed to realize who the ground first of all belonged to. This ground did not totally belong to this rich man but it belonged to the Lord. The scripture tells us that this man was already rich before he even planted these crops. There is nothing wrong with being rich as long as our riches don't have us. As long as we don't put riches before God and start serving them instead of serving God. This man had more than enough fruit. Verse 17 explains that after seeing all of this increase he thought about no one but himself. "And he thought within himself, saying, What shall I do, because I have no room where to bestow my fruits?" This man did not thank God for the fruits nor did he acknowledge God about what to do with such great harvest. This man was self centered. He only thought about his other companions who were me, myself, and I.

There is no doubt that this man did put in much time, energy, and money into this ground. But what he failed to realize was that it was God who gave the increase. It was God who blessed this man's ground in order for him to be a blessing to others. Verse 18, "and he said, this will I do; I will pull down my barns and build greater; and there will I bestow all my fruits and my goods". Verse 19, "And I will say to my soul, soul, thou hast much goods laid up for many years; take thine ease, eat, drink, and be merry". What this man did is what many people are still doing today. He made his heaven here on earth. He was living here on earth as thou he did not have to die. He was living as if this world was the final resting place for this body and soul. He said, I will say to my soul you have much laid up, you have much put back for the future. Your life is secure. You have no problems now, nor will you have any in the future. So kick back, take it easy, eat whatever you want to eat. Drink whatever you want to drink and be happy! Verse 20, "But God said unto him, Thou fool, this night thy soul shall be required of thee: then whose shall those things be which thou hast provided?" What should be noticed here is that God Almighty saw everything

2

that this man was doing and he heard everything that this man was saying. God also saw the motives of this man's heart. All God saw was self motivation and greed. Then God began to speak and let this man know just how things were going to be and who was really in charge. When God begins to speak or take action on something, nothing or nobody can stop Him. God was letting this man know that this was foolish of him to center his life only around material things and never consider God or his soul. God told this man not tomorrow, not next week, not next month, but <u>THIS</u> night your life will come to a sudden <u>END</u>. This night your soul will be ushered to it's eternal destination. Then after you are dead and buried, I want to know who will all of those things belong to? You will not be able to take any of them out of this world with you which you have provided for someone else. Again, my question to you is as you read this book, "WHAT ABOUT YOUR SOUL?" This man no doubt had not heard what Job said in Job chapter one and verse twenty one, "Naked came I out of my mothers womb, and naked shall I return thither.

<u>Verse 21</u>, The Lord concluded here by saying "So is he that layeth up treasure for himself, and is not rich toward God". We must never allow ourselves to live in this world as though this is it, because this is not all of it. We need to daily give God some of our time, energy, and resources every time the opportunity presents itself. Job 1:1-3, speaks of a godly man who was rich with material things and rich toward God also. <u>Verse 1</u>, "There was a man in the land of Uz, whose name was Job. And that man was perfect and upright and one that feared God, and eschewed evil". This does not mean that Job was sinless. What this verse is saying is that Job's heart, his desires, his actions; his only will was to do the will of God. Job was very mature in the Lord. He knew what God expected and he tried daily with all of his heart to please God. Job also knew what the Lord did not want him to do. And he strived with all of his heart not to do it. Job was upright, meaning that he walked with God. He lived not just one day for the Lord on a Sunday morning, but he lived 365 days a year for the Lord. He honored God. All that appeared to be evil, Job stayed away from it. No matter who took part in doing the evil, Job still had no part in it. What a very good example for us to follow today. Job was a wealthy man. <u>Verse 2</u>, "And there were born unto him seven sons and three daughters". This man was blessed by God to have a big family. <u>Verse 3</u> tells us that Job was blessed with

seven thousand sheep, three thousand camels, five hundred yoke of oxen, five hundred she asses, and a very great household. Job was rich but at the same time Job's riches did not have him. Instead the Lord had Job's <u>whole heart</u>. This man was a good example of someone who was rich toward God. Abraham is another man who was rich toward God. <u>Genesis 13:2</u> tells us that Abram was very rich in cattle, in silver, and in gold. Still Abram had his priorities right with God. So we can see clearly that God has no problem with us having wealth, as long as we don't put the wealth before God. If we allow this to be, then our wealth will then become our god. Then we will end up just as the rich man whose ground brought forth plenty. We will forget about our soul and end up being separated eternally from God.

The Lord has told us in <u>Luke 12:29-31</u>, "And seek not ye what ye shall eat or what ye shall drink neither be ye of doubtful mind. For all these things do the nations of the world seek after: and your Father knoweth that ye have need of these things. But rather seek ye the kingdom of God; And all these things shall be added unto you". When we put God first we will not have to chase after material things, but God will cause material things to chase after us. Let us put God first all the days of our lives. Then after we leave this walk of life our soul will be welcomed into God's presence to live eternally with God and not separated eternally away from God.

CHAPTER TWO

Two Eternal Places For Our Soul

Luke 16:19-13 speaks about two places that our soul will spend eternity after we die. The choice is up to us where we want to spend eternity. Verse 19, "There was a certain rich man, which was clothed in purple and fine linen, and fared sumptuously everyday". This man wore nothing but the best of clothing, and not only did he believe in wearing the best when it came down to clothes, but this man also believed in eating the best of food and drinking the best drinks money could buy. Verse 20, "And there was a certain beggar named Lazarus, which was laid at this gate, full of sores". Here we have two men. One was in the best of health and had more than enough. And one who was in bad physical health and on top of that he had nothing to eat. Lazarus, because of his physical condition, was forced to beg for a living. Begging was not something that he did because he wanted to, but he was a beggar because of these unwanted circumstances in his life. Sometimes we will have to do things that we really don't want to do because of certain unwanted circumstances. Not only was Lazarus a beggar but he was also paralyzed. He could not walk. He was helpless. He had to wait on someone to come and carry him where he needed to go. Lazarus was carried by others and laid at the gate or entrance way of what appeared to be this rich man's mansion. Not only was Lazarus was a beggar and a paraplegic, but he was also sick. His body was full of sores. These sores were no doubt left unattended due to the lack of money. These sores had to have been full of infections which means if there was infection present, then there had to also be fever. And if there was fever, his entire body was severely weak. <u>Verse 21</u>, "And desiring to be fed with the crumbs which fell from the rich man's table; moreover the dogs came and licked his sores". Lazarus did not have a big desire which was impossible to fulfill. But he had a very small desire. He did not even desire to have a piece of bread. But all he wanted was the crumbs from the bread which are usually gathered up and thrown into the trash. This was all that the beggar was asking for, the crumbs which fell from the rich man's table. As Lazarus laid there helpless at the gate, the dogs came where he was and showed more compassion to the beggar than the rich man. When these dogs came to the place where Lazarus was, they did not attack him, which they could have easily done. This man was unable to move or fight them off. The Lord caused these dogs to show up with the right spirit. When they came to Lazarus, they didn't attach him but instead brought him comfort. When they came to where Lazarus was, they began to not bite him but lick his sores. These dogs brought more relief to this hungry, sick, helpless man than the rich man did. Whenever we have the chance to help someone, we need to be found doing so.

<u>Verse 22</u>, "And it came to pass, that the beggar died, and was carried by angels into Abraham's bosom". All of his begging days were over. All of his hungry days were over. What should be notice here also is after the beggar died, life did not totally end for him. His physical body died, but his spiritual man, his soul, was still alive. His soul was then carried not by one angel, but his soul was carried by *angels* into Abraham's bosom (representing the presence of God). As time continued to move on, the rich man also died and was buried. And his soul lived on also after his physical death. But there is no mention of any angels carrying him anywhere. He was not taken into Abraham's bosom. The scripture says he died and was buried. <u>Verse 23</u>, "And in hell he lift up his eyes, being in torments, and seeth Abraham afar off, and Lazarus in this bosom". We find here that after this rich, self centered man died, his soul went to hell to spend eternity. While in hell, he began to look around and as he looked around he came to the conclusion that he couldn't get any help from anyone in hell so he began to look up out of hell. While in hell, his soul was in torment. He was suffering in agony more than just one way. As he began to look up out of hell, he was able to see Abraham from a far distance. He kept on looking until he was able to see Lazarus, the same man that he paid no

attention to when he was alive on earth. As he looked, he saw Lazarus in a much better position than he was in. He then noticed that Lazarus was now in a position to help him. <u>Verse 24</u>, "And he cried and said, Father Abraham, have mercy on me and send Lazarus that he may dip the tip of his finger in water and cool my tongue; for I am tormented in this flame". There is an old saying that has been said down through the years which goes: Be very careful how you treat people on your way up the ladder of success because you may need them one day if you happen to fall from the top of the ladder on your way back down. As this man's soul was being tormented in hell, he began to cry out, but it was too late to cry. If we allow our soul to end up in hell, it will be too late for us to cry also. This man cried out asking Abraham for what he could not give him and that was relief. The same relief that he himself refused to give to Lazarus when he had countless opportunities to do so. He cried out for mercy and not only did he cry out for mercy, but he also asked Abraham's permission to send him some help from the same person that he overlooked and would not help. He asked Abraham to send Lazarus, the same man that he thought he would never need any help from. He asked Abraham if Lazarus could come and dip not his hand but just the tip of one of his fingers in some water and bring it to him. He told Abraham that he was being tormented in the flames. This should let us know that every time we have an opportunity to do good, to help someone who we know are in great need, we should be found going out of our way and go the extra mile to help them. Life is very uncertain. We can be up today, doing good and feeling well, but by night fall we could be gone out of this world and ushered into eternity. *WHAT ABOUT YOUR SOUL?*

CHAPTER THREE

Hell, A Place Where Outside Help Is Not Allowed

We are going to find out here that this man needed help but he was in a place where he would spend eternity and still couldn't get any outside mercy or help. Verse 25, "But Abraham said, son, remember that thou in thy lifetime receivedst thy good things, and likewise Lazarus evil things: but now he is comforted and thou art tormented". Abraham brought back to this man's remembrance what he seemed to have quickly forgotten. He reminded him of that very good lifestyle that he had lived when he was on earth. Then he was reminded of how Lazarus the beggar, the hungry man, received the evil things of life. Then Abraham brought him up to the present state that he was now in. Abraham told him but now Lazarus' suffering days are now over, but yours have just begun. Your suffering will be FOREVER. There will be no changes. This man's soul suffered eternally and there was never any relief for him. Verse 26, "And beside all this, between us and you there is a great gulf fixed: so that they which would pass from hence to you cannot; neither can they pass to us, that would come from thence". Abraham went on to tell this hopeless soul that between Lazarus, myself, and you, the Lord has it fixed so that they cannot come together. There is a great space fixed, a great separation fixed so that those who want to pass from us to you cannot do so. Neither can those who are where you are can come to us. Again, hell is a place where outside help is not allowed. Abraham was letting this man know, where Lazarus and I are, we are here for eternity. And where you are, you are there for eternity. There has been no mistake and there will be no changes. Verse 27, "Then he said, I pray thee therefore, Father that thou wouldest send him to my father's house". When this man saw that there was no hope for him to be delivered, he then thought about those who were still alive, walking around on earth in his family who had a chance to escape this terrible place that he ended up in. He asked Abraham then if he couldn't get any help for himself, if he would send Lazarus back to the earth to his father's house to warn those who were in his family to not end up where he was. He wanted to warn them before they died to please not come here where I am. <u>Verse 28</u>, "For I have five brethren that he may testify unto them, lest they also come into this place of torment". These five brothers no doubt were living the same lifestyle that this man had lived all of his life. He wanted them to be warned that they needed to change their lifestyle and to not just be focused on the material things and make preparation while they were on earth to secure the right place for their soul to spend eternity. Otherwise they would end up in the same undesired place called hell where he was. This was his choice. He was not forced to be where he was. But he was there because of many wrong choices that he had made. <u>Verse 29</u>, "Abraham saith unto him, they have Moses and the prophets, let them hear him. Abraham told this man that God had already put people on earth who were chosen, anointed, and appointed by God that he would use as his mouthpiece to speak through. God is still speaking today but the problem is, people are too busy living the life that they want to live. The cares of this present world have many to the point of thinking that they don't have time for God or the church. It's sad but it's true. The only time that some people think about God is when they are in a situation where no one can get them out of but God. Then as soon as they are delivered they will walk away from God, until they find themselves in another bad situation that they again can't get themselves out of. God is still speaking. The question is, are we listening and taking heed to what He is saying to us? The Lord is saying the same thing to us today and that is let us hear and obey those who the Lord has chosen to be a mouthpiece for Him. Then our eternal end will be a happy ending. <u>Verse 30</u>, "And he said, nay, Father Abraham; but if one went unto them from the dead, they will repent". Even though all hope was gone for this man's soul, he was still determined to do all that he could do to get some vital information back to his lost brothers before it was too late. He still tried to convince Abraham that if he allowed Lazarus to return back to earth and warn his brothers, surely they would repent and turn away from that lifestyle they were living.

Verse 31, "And he said unto them, if they hear not Moses and the prophets, neither will they be persuaded, though one rose from the dead". Abrahams conclusion was to let this hopeless, lost soul know again that God had the last say so about this situation and that God had already fixed this for every soul. While people are alive on earth, all a person has to do is accept Jesus Christ as their personal Savior and give their lives to Him on this side of life. Then when death comes, all it will do is bring them into the eternal presence of God. And there, their soul will spend eternity. Abraham told this rich man, if they refuse to hear God's chosen, who are alive and walking round on earth with them, then they would not be persuaded to do any better by someone who had been sent back from the dead. Remember, no one can send you to hell but you. It's a choice. *WHAT ABOUT YOUR SOUL?*

CHAPTER FOUR

It's God's Will That Everyone Be Saved

It's not God's will that any man perish and his soul be lost. According to 2 Peter 3:9, "The Lord is not slack concerning His promise as some men count slackness; But is longsuffering to us-ward, not willing that any should perish, but that all should come to repentance". The promise that the apostle Peter is talking about here is the one that the apostle Paul wrote about in Romans 10:9, "that if thou shalt confess with thy mouth, the Lord Jesus and shalt believe in thine heart that God hath raised Him, Jesus from the dead, thou salt be saved". Then the apostle Peter goes on to let us know that God is long-suffering, which means that God is a God of great patience. God will continue to spare a persons life even when they are living in constant, unrepented sin. The reason why God does this is because it's not God's will that anyone should die and their soul end up eternally separated from God. It's God's will that every human being on the face of this earth repent and turn from their way of living in sin and turn to God's way of living which leads to eternal life and not eternal damnation. The unsaved, those who have not accepted Jesus as their personal Savior, need to know that God does not hate them, but God loves them. John 3:16 says, "For God so loved the world that He gave His only begotten So, that whosoever believeth in Him should not perish, but have everlasting life". Since we know now that it's not God's will that anyone should perish, this leaves no one but Satan. It's the devil's will that we all die in our sin and our soul end up eternally separated from God. Our God speaks again about His great concern for man's soul through Ezekiel in Ezekiel

18:21-23, "But if the wicked will turn from all his sins that he hath committed and keep all my statutes and do that which is lawful and right, he shall surely live, he shall not die". All the Lord is saying here is, if the sinner, the unsaved, will give up their way of living and doing things and turn to the Lord and allow Him to teach them how to live for Him and do what is right. The Lords says that they shall live eternally and not die. I often find myself telling people, if the Lord saved me, He can and He will save anybody, if they will turn from their sins and turn to the Lord and allow Him to save them. Before I turned to the Lord, I was living deep in sin. I didn't know how to come out of living that way until I went back to church after staying out for many years. I began to change my heart and my way of thinking because God's word began to renew my mind as I received it. Then the Lord began to work in my life through His Holy Spirit. He moved me from sitting on the last pew in the church to singing in the choir. Then from the choir to a deacon on the deacon board. Then to a Sunday school teacher and superintendent. On November 12, 1989, the Lord called me to preach the gospel. March 20, 1993, I was called to Pastor some of God's sheep and I'm still pastoring at this time. So I know from experience, if a person has a will to change and give up their way of living and turn to the Lord, I'm a living witness that He will bring them up and out of their sin and lead them into His way of righteousness. All over this world people are trying to find the answer to whatever it is they are dealing with. Still they have not found the answer yet. They have been looking in the wrong places. They have been passing by the answer, no doubt, everyday. They need to know that the answer to whatever it is they are going through is in the church. Jesus is the answer.

Verse 22, "And all his transgressions that he hath committed they shall not be mentioned unto him; In his righteousness that he hath done shall he live". Our God is the same yesterday, today, and forever. He does not change. People will change. Many of them are just like the weather, you never know what to expect from them. Thank God that He is not like this. If God was willing to forgive and forget the wickedness of those who truly turned to Him with a true heart during the time of Ezekiel, then God is still patiently waiting on the wicked to repent and live today. Instead of blaming the human being for their wickedness, we need to blame the one who is the source of the problem, Satan. Years ago when I was living a sinful life, I wanted to stop. I had a desire to stop but I couldn't because I couldn't deliver myself. Each time I tried, I only got worse. I realize now that those were evil spirits that had me bound until one day, I cried out to God. I told the Lord, I give up and I asked Him to help me. From that hour all the way up to this present moment, the Lord has and He is still helping me. Now He's waiting on you to cry out to Him and ask Him to help you. Go ahead and ask Him.

Verse 23, "Have I any pleasure at all that the wicked should die? Saith the Lord God; And that he should return from his ways and live?" Satan has deceived many people into thinking that all God does is sit on His righteous throne in heaven and wait for someone to do wrong so that He can cut them down on the spot. Our God does not operate in this manner. God is a loving God. He is forgiving and He is merciful. He is also a God of righteousness. God gets no pleasure out of seeing a soul separated from Him eternally, which is eternal damnation. It's God's will that the wicked forsake their ways and the unrighteous man his thoughts. God wants all souls to live eternally with Him. The choice is up to us. We determine where our soul will spend eternity by the lifestyle we choose to live everyday of our lives. We saw in the earlier part of this book that this is what happened to the two men. They made the choice themselves where they would spend eternity by the way they lived. The same thing is true with us. Where will we spend eternity? Just as we must prepare to live, we must prepare to die.

CHAPTER FIVE

We Brought Nothing In, We Carry Nothing Out

The Lord said in Haggai 2:8, "The silver is mine, and the gold is mine, saith the Lord of hosts". If the silver and gold belonged to the Lord during the time of Haggai the prophet, guess what? It still belongs to the Lord today, nothing has changed. King David wrong in Psalm 24:1, "The earth is the Lord's and the fullness thereof; the world, and they that dwell therein". These scriptures are telling us that everything and everybody here on earth belongs to the Lord. Whatever we have now, it will all one day return back to the rightful owner, who is the Lord. It is the Lord who allowed us to be blessed with some of these material blessings. By and by as time goes on, one out of two things will happen. Number one: These material things may be taken away from us due to some unwanted circumstances. Number two: We will die and leave them all behind for someone else to have for just a little while.

The apostle Paul also lets us know in 1 Timothy 6:7, "For we brought noting into this world, and it is certain we can carry nothing out". Never in the history of this world has anyone been born into this world with money wrapped around their arms or legs, or holding silver or gold in their hands as they were birthed into this world. Even if they are born into a wealthy family, they were still born into this world with nothing. Since they came here with nothing, Paul goes on to let us know, it's a fact that after they die, they will carry nothing out. No armored truck filled with money, silver, or gold has ever been driven to a graveyard and buried alone side anyone. If this has ever happened, I'm sure it didn't stay there long before someone came along and found a way to get the money out. Verse 8, "And having food and raiment let us be therewith content". If the Lord is providing us with food, clothing, shelter over our heads, and supplying all of our basic needs, then we ought to be thankful and be content with what we have until the Lord opens greater doors for us to have more. There are so many people all over this world who have no food to eat, no clean water to drink, no house to come into out of the cold, heat or rain. They have no transportation. They have to walk miles to get where they need to go. But the amazing thing about this is, they are more thankful and happy than those who have these things. The ones who have been blessed with these things are complaining and unthankful. Many people go wrong when they step out on their own and try to do it all on their own without God. When this happens, God has been left out. Then things become more important than the Lord. We must always keep this in mind, for we brought nothing into this world and it is certain we can carry nothing out. Jesus said in Matthew 6:19-21, "Lay not up for yourselves treasures upon earth, where moth and rust doth corrupt, and where thieves break through and steal: For where your treasure is, there will your heart be also". 1 Timothy 6:9 warns us to be very careful. "But they that will be rich fall into temptation and a snare, and into many foolish and hurtful lusts, which drown men in destruction and perdition". Here Paul is talking about those who set out in life with a one track mind and that is to get rich as soon as possible. They care nothing about who they have to walk on, hurt, or deceive to get there. They end up doing many harmful and hurtful things to themselves and others. They only lust for the power of money then down through the years, they end up being destroyed by the power of greed. Instead of them being the master of their money, their money becomes their master. There is nothing wrong with being rich, as long as we are not controlled by these riches. Verse 10, "For the love of money is the root of all evil: which while some coveted after, they have erred from the faith, and pierced themselves through with many sorrows". It's a blessing to have money and have plenty of it. It's God's will that we prosper and be in health even as our soul prospers. Without money, we will not be able to do anything. Ecclesiastes 10:19 reads, "A feast is made for laughter, and wine maketh merry: but money answereth all things". Money answers all material things. There are still many things that money cannot answer for. (1) Real peace of mind which only comes through a person relationship with the Lord. (2) Real inside joy which will be present when all our money is gone. Jesus Christ is the only one who can give us this inside joy. This joy I have the world didn't give it to me and the world can't take it away. Again, God has no problem at all with us having money and plenty of it. But God does have a problem when we allow money to have us. When money has us we are then controlled by it and will be found doing whatever it takes to keep money flowing, whether we are right or wrong. It's sad but it's true. There are many people today who will even kill just to receive money. This is a good example of the love for money. This love for money didn't just begin in our generation but this has been happening all the way back in the biblical days. The love for money will bring many sorrows into our lives. Judas, one of the Lord's chosen disciples, had a love for money because he betrayed Jesus for thirty pieces of silver. After Judas saw that he was condemned and that he had betrayed innocent blood, he went out and hanged himself Matthew 27:3-5. The love for money will cause people to loose much needed sleep at night. When we put God first and seek His kingdom and His righteousness, God has promised us that all these things shall be added unto us. No good things will the Lord withhold from them that walk upright. When we put God first, we won't have to worry about money because God will give us one thought and cause that thought to be turned into a multi-million dollar idea. As we take care of God's business, God will take care of our business. As we delight ourselves in the Lord, He will give us the desires of our heart because nothing is too hard for the Lord, nothing. The number one thing we need to keep in mind is where will our soul spend eternity and one day Jesus is coming back. Will we be ready to meet Him? No man knows the day nor the hour when the Lord will return. The Lord has told us to be ye also ready. Don't get ready, be ready!

CHAPTER SIX

Jesus Is Coming Back

We must always keep in mind that one day the Lord will return and He did not tell us to get ready, but He told us to be ye also ready. Act 1:9-11 tells us the He's gone but he's coming back. Verse 9, "And when he had spoken of these things, while they beheld, he was taken up; and a cloud received him out of their sight". After Jesus had finished speaking to his disciples promising them Divine Power to be effective witnesses, as they stood there looking at him, a cloud carried Him up and out of their sight. Notice the scripture says He was carried up. When our load seems as though it is too heavy for us to bear, we need to look up and ask the Lord to help us. Verse 10, "And while they look steadfastly toward heaven as He went up, behold, two men stood by him in white apparel". As the Lord was taken up and out of the disciple's sight, this no doubt had their total attention. They were looking only one way and that was up toward heaven, the same way that Jesus went. When trouble comes into our lives, we too are to look only one way and that way is up toward heaven because this is where our problem solver is. David said "I will lift up mine eyes unto the hills, from whence cometh my help. My help cometh from the Lord, which made heaven and earth" Psalm 121:1-2. As Jesus was taken up into heaven, two angels in the form of men came and stood by the disciples as they looked up toward heaven. Our bible also tells us to be careful of how we entertain strangers, for we may be entertaining God sent angels unaware. Those angels were sent from God with a message for these men of God. Also, they were dressed in white clothing symbolizing purity. Verse 11, "Which also said, ye men of Galilee, why stand ye gazing up into heaven? This same Jesus, which is taken up from you into heaven, shall so come in like manner as ye have seen him go into heaven". These two angels asked a question, and then they gave these men of God some divine future revelation. These angels knew what area these disciples had come from because they called them men of Galilee. They also asked them why they were standing there in a trance looking up into heaven. They told these disciples not another one, but this same Jesus who is gone back into heaven, one day He's coming back the same way that you have seen him go into heaven. In other words, He's gone but one day He's coming back. When Jesus comes back, will you and I return back into heaven with him? *WHAT ABOUT YOUR SOUL?*

Matthew 24:34-42 talks about the second coming of our Lord and Savior Jesus Christ. Verse 36, "But of that day and hour knoweth no man, no, not the angels of heaven, but my Father only". Jesus is saying here that the day and hour in which he will return, no man knows this. No matter how much a person may claim he does, Jesus has said that NO man knows this. Even the angels in heaven with God don't know this. God has not revealed this to any man or angel. No one knows when Jesus will return for those who have accepted Him as their personal Savior. I don't know about you, but I am determined to be ready when Jesus returns for all those who have accepted Him as their personal Savior. If someone tells us that they are coming by to pick us up, at that time they never give us the exact time they will be coming. The best thing for us to do to keep from missing them is to get ready and be ready and watching for them until we see them pull up in the driveway. We get ready by accepting Jesus as our personal Savior and we stay ready by us being born again. Our mind and heart must be renewed and regenerated with God's word, love, and Holy Spirit. Verse 37, "But as the days of Noah were, so shall also the coming of the son of man be". Even though we don't know the exact day or hour that our Lord will return, in this verse the Lord does give us a clue. He lets us know here that there will be a repeat. The same things that were going on during the time of Noah before the flood came, will repeat themselves before the son of God comes again.

Verse 38, "For as in the days that were before the flood they were eating and drinking, marrying and giving in marriage until the day Noah entered into the ark". As we look around in this world in which we live, we can see that the exact things that were going on during the time of Noah before the flood, are repeating themselves in our day and time. Before the Lord sent the flood, people were eating whatever they wanted to eat. They were drinking whatever they wanted to drink. They were all having a good time day and night. They were exchanging wives and husbands with each other. All of these things went on continually all the way up until the same day that Noah and those with him went into the ark. Only those inside of the ark were saved. All those on the outside of the ark died. My question to you is, "Are you in the ark or are you on the outside of the ark?" The ark I'm talking about is the ark of safety which is only in Jesus Christ. To get into this ark, all we have to do is confess with our mouth the Lord Jesus and believe in our heart that God has raised him from the dead. This then places us in the Lord's ark of safety until the Lord returns for us. Now that we are in the ark, we are to live for the Lord daily. Verse 39, "And knew not until the flood came, and took them all away; so shall also the coming of the son of man be". Jesus said here that those who lived in their unrepented sins and enjoyed this all the way up to the completion of the ark did not make it into the ark. They did not recognize what was going on until it was too late. When the flood showed up, it was too late. Even before the flood came, the unsaved still had time to repent and turn to the Lord because after Noah completed the ark, the unsaved still had at least 39 days to turn to the Lord. Before the flood came, it rained forty days and forty nights before the flood was complete. They had a chance to get it right instead they made a choice to keep on sinning all the way up until the flood came and took them all away. Jesus has said the same thing will happen during the second coming of Christ. This time it will not be water but with fire. Please don't let the Lord come back and you are not ready. PLEASE BE READY!

Verse 40, "Then shall two be in the field; the one shall be taken and the other left". When the Lord comes back, people will be found working on their jobs. The one that shall be taken up is the one who has accepted Jesus as their personal Savior and has lived for the Lord during their lifetime. Then one that shall be left behind is the one who rejected Jesus, the unbeliever, the one who lived his or her life as they pleased. The one who started out with the Lord but turned back into the world will be the one who will be left behind. I don't know about you, but I don't like being left behind and this is one time that I refuse to be left behind. I am determined to not be left behind. What about you?

Verse 41, "Two women shall be grinding at the mill; the one shall be taken, and the other left". Here we have two women working on a job doing the same kind of work, but they are living two kinds of daily lifestyles. One is saved and the other one is not saved. The one who is saved will be taken up, taken up out of this world of suffering and trouble to live eternally with the Lord. Then again, the one who is not saved, the one who did not accept Jesus as her personal Savior will be left behind. I don't know about you. I can only speak for myself. I am determined not to be left behind. It's no fun at all to be left behind especially during the second coming of Christ.

Verse 42, "Watch therefore: for ye know not what hour your Lord doth come". Since you and I don't know what hour that our Lord will return, the best thing for us to do daily is to watch and live each day in expectation, expecting the Lord to return at anytime. We need to watch daily what we do and say. Watch daily how we treat people. We need to watch daily and make sure that we take time to pray and forgive our brothers and sisters. It makes no difference if they are saved in the church or a sinner in the world. We need to watch and make sure that we are merciful to all that need mercy. And above all, we need to watch and make sure that we love one another, even our enemies. Love is greater than hate. Those who love are of God. God is love. Will our soul be ready for the second coming of our Lord and Savior Jesus Christ?

1 Thessalonians 4:16-18, the apostle Paul writes about the second coming of Christ. Verse 16, "For the Lord himself shall descend from heaven with a shout, with the voice of the archangel, and with the trump of God: and the dead in Christ shall rise first". Paul is letting us know here that one day, the Lord himself will return. He will not send any angel, prophet, apostle, evangelist, pastor or teacher. But Jesus Christ himself will appear from heaven. The Lord will then shout with the voice of the archangel, the most powerful of all the angels in heaven. This shout will be so powerful, that it's going to wake up all the dead sleeping Christians who died in Christ. The dead in Christ will be resurrected from the grave by that same power that resurrected Jesus from the tomb. Verse 17, "Then we which are alive and remain shall be caught up together with them in the clouds, to meet the Lord in the air:

and so shall we ever be with the Lord". All those who will be alive, have accepted the Lord as their personal Savior, have been born again, and are living down here on earth will be caught up. They will be rapture up and taken up out of this world and will be joined together with the resurrected dead, those raised from the grave. We will meet the Lord in the air. After meeting the Lord, there will be no more separation. We will live eternally with the Lord. There will be no more good byes or I will see you tomorrow or next week or next year. Instead, we will live eternally together with the Lord. Verse 18, "Wherefore comfort one another with these words". Whatever you may be going through right now, no matter how hard it may seem to be on you, if you will allow Him to, God will comfort you with His divine peace. And right in the middle of that problem, God will give you rest. Be encouraged, whatever you may be going through and no matter how long you've been in that situation, the Lord told me to tell you, it's only temporary. It's only for a set season. It will change. Believe that it's going to change. It changed for King David. That's why he said, "Weeping may endure for a night, but joy cometh in the morning" Psalm 30:5. So cheer up. Be of good courage and motivate yourself knowing that the Lord will keep His word. Heaven and earth shall pass away but God's word shall not pass away. Get rooted and grounded in God's words. On Sunday, be found in Sunday school and morning worship. On Wednesday night, be found in mid-week prayer and bible study.

CHAPTER SEVEN

One On One With God

In the book of Revelation chapter 1:9-10, John, one of the Lord's apostles, said, I John was in the Isle called Patmos. John said that he was put out there for two reasons; the first reason was for the word of God. Preaching the gospel of Jesus Christ had gotten John into trouble. The preaching of the gospel of Jesus Christ is still getting God's chosen in trouble today. The second reason that John was on the Isle called Patmos was for the testimony of Jesus Christ. As John talked about the birth, death, burial, and resurrection of Jesus, this got him into much trouble. There were those who were in authority and who did not believe in John or his preaching. There are still many people all over this world who still do not believe.

Verse 10, John goes on to say, "I was in the spirit on the Lord's day, and heard behind me a great voice, as of a trumpet". The devil thought that he had done away with John for good when he worked through the religious leaders who decided that they would put John out of society and put him out on this Isle all by himself. When we walk with God with a pure heart, God will never leave us nor forsake us. Some of God's greatest revelations are given to us when we are all alone by ourselves, ONE ON ONE WITH GOD. These are the times when the Lord can and will really speak to us. John was caught up in the spirit of God. John said I was in the spirit of God, I heard a voice behind me, a great voice, sounding like that of a trumpet. This voice no doubt got John's total attention. You can see the Lord cannot really speak to us the way that He wants to until He has our total attention.

The question that needs to be asked and answered is. "Does the Lord have our total attention? Before God called Moses to go back to Egypt and bring the children of Israel out, the first thing that the Lord did was get Moses' total attention through the burning bush, which burned but never burned up. The only way that the Lord can get our total attention is that we too must get away from certain people and get off by ourselves, then the Lord will speak to us too. In Revelation 20:11-15, the Lord told John to write about the second resurrection because the first resurrection will be the resurrection of the church that Paul talked about when he said the dead in Christ shall rise first, 1 Thessalonians 4:16. Revelation 20:6 backs this up when the Lord told John to write, "blessed and holy is he that hath part in the first resurrection: on such the second death hath no power". The second death that John is talking about here is the lake of fire.

Revelation 20:10 lets us know what the devil's end will be. Verse 10, "And the devil that deceived them was cast into the lake of fire and brimstone, where the beast and the false prophet are, and shall be tormented day and night for ever and ever". Please answer this question now before you die. WHAT ABOUT YOUR SOUL? The devil, the same one who deceived Eve and Adam in the garden of Eden, is still deceiving people today even more all over this world. When this world comes to an end, the Lord will do away with the devil forever. He will be thrown into the lake of fire where demons and all the false prophets will already be. The Lord has told us to beware of the false prophets who will come to us in sheep's clothing, but inwardly in their hearts they are ravening wolves. False prophets have trained themselves to walk like a real prophet, but all the time they are false, pretenders, and deceivers sent straight from the devils camp. The devil, his demons, and all the false prophets after they are thrown into the lake of fire, will be tormented day and night. There will be no end to their torment. Not only will the devil and the false prophets be cast into the lake of fire, but all liars, the wicked, the evil doers, the workers of iniquity, and all unbelievers will be cast into the lake of fire after the second resurrection. All those who end up in the lake of fire will be there because it was their choice and not God's. It was their final decision, not God's.

Revelation 20:12-15, verse12, "And I saw the dead, small and great, stand before God; and the books were opened: and another book was opened, which is the book of life: and the dead were judged out of those things which were written in the books, according to their works". While on the Isle called Patmos, the Lord allowed John to see what the end of the unsaved would be. John said, I saw the dead, small and great. In other words, I saw those who were not known world wide along with those who were know world wide. I saw the uneducated and I saw the well educated, I saw the poor and I saw the rich. They all stood before God Almighty to be judged. No one will be able to escape. John said the books were opened. In those books will be people's lifetime records, all that they did will be in the books. All that they did not confess and repent of will be written in the books. If anyone died with hatred in their heart, it will be written in the books. All unrepented sin will be written in the books. This judgment day will be the final roll call and everyone will have to answer for themselves. John said, "and another book was opened, which is the book of life". In this book will be the names of all those who have received eternal, everlasting life. The resurrected dead will be judged according to the things written in the books. They will be judged according to what they have done and what they did not do, according to the word of God. What we need to realize here, is that people are the one who will be responsible for the things that will be written in the books, not God. All God has done was kept a perfect record. People are the ones who made the record.

Verse 13, "And the sea gave up the dead which were in it; and death and hell delivered up the dead which were in them: and they were judged every man according to their works". During this great judgment, all those who died at sea will be resurrected. They will stand before the throne of God to be judged. All those who died and did not accept Jesus as their personal Savior, also those in hell will be resurrected from the dead. They will stand before God and will be judged according to their works, according to the lifestyle they have lived when they were alive on earth. They will not be judged for something that someone else has done, but they will be judged according to all the things that they themselves have done. After death and hell have delivered up all those whom they were holding, then God will do away with death and hell. They both will be thrown into the lake of fire.

Verse 14, "And death and hell were cast into the lake of fire. This is the second death". The first death is the death of the physical man. The second death is the death of the spiritual man. I trust that you are able to say the same thing, I thank God that I'm saved and I don't have to be concerned about the second death. Now I need to know are you saved? If you are not, please accept Jesus Christ as your personal Savior now before it's too late. All you have to do is do what I did and what countless of others have done and that is to surrender. Give up your way of living and open your heart and invite Jesus to come in and take total control of your life. The Lord is standing at the door of your heart knocking. Don't you hear Him? Open up and let Him in.

Verse 15, "And whosoever was not found written in the book of life was cast into the lake of fire". All those who rejected the Lord, all those who did not accept Jesus as their personal Savior, all those who never repented and lived the lifestyle that they wanted to live, names will not be found in the book of eternal life. Souls will be cast into the lake of fire which is the eternal second death, the eternal death of the soul. During this final judgment, all those who thought they had gotten away, will find out that they had only gotten by for a while. No one will be able to get by, no one will be able to get away. It makes no difference how poor or wealthy a person has been, things or money will not be able to help them. Knowing Jesus will be the only thing that will make the difference during this final judgment. Before you die, make sure that you know that your name is written in the Lamb's Book of Life. In the lake of fire there will be no second chances. In the lake of fire there will be no mercy. In the lake of fire there will be no grace. In the lake of fire it will be too late to confess sins or repent. And finally, in the lake of fire, there will be no more time because time will be replaced by eternity. *WHAT ABOUT YOUR SOUL?*

Revelation 22:11-12 is saying when the Lord comes back, whatever type of lifestyle we are living, when Jesus reappears on the cloud, don't try to change because it will be too late. Again, please don't let it be too late for you. Verse 11, "He that is unjust, let him be unjust still: and he which is filthy, let him be filthy still: and he that is righteous, let him be righteous still: and he that is holy, let him be holy still". What the Lord is saying here is, when He comes back, all those who will be caught living a lifestyle, He is saying to them, don't try to change then because it will be too late. Just continue on being unjust when they look up and see the Lord coming on the clouds with great power and with great glory. All those who were living filthy lifestyles are told not to change because it will be too late. Continue to be filthy. These who are righteous, walking upright in the Lord with all their heart, soul, mind, and strength are told to continue to be righteous when the Lord descends from heaven. Those who are holy are told not to change but to continue living holy lives. People have allowed Satan to convince them into thinking that no one can live a holy life. He has even convinced many Christians into thinking, believing, and confessing this also. We must always keep this in mind, that the devil is the author of deception. He is a liar from the beginning and he will continue to be one all the way up until he is cast into the lake of fire. The Lord has said be ye holy for I am holy. If this was not possible for us to do, the Lord would have never told us to do it. No, we cannot be holy on our own, but when we submit to the holy spirit, the greater one on the inside of us, He then takes the driver seat and He enables us to live holy. Without the Holy Spirit living through us in the eyesight of God, all of our righteousness is as filthy rags. The only way that you and I can be holy is that we must be filled with God's Holy Spirit. When this happens, it is no longer us doing the living but God's Holy Spirit. So when we hear the word holy, we don't have to be afraid or panic. The more submitted we are to the Holy Spirit, the more holy our lifestyle will be for the Lord and others to see.

CHAPTER EIGHT

Payday Is Coming

<u>Revelation 22:12</u>, "And, behold, I come quickly; and my reward is with me, to give every man according as his works shall be". The Lord told John to let us know, He's coming in a hurry. His coming will be so swift that all those who have not repented will not have time to do so. The Lord's coming will be so swift that all those who will not be living right will not have time to get right. So now is the time to turn from all evil, unrighteousness, wickedness, and turn to the Lord with all of your heart and allow the Lord to come into our lives and live through us daily. Not only will the Lord come quickly but when He comes back, He will also bring our rewards with Him and He will give to everyone of us according to the works we have done. If we have done all evil, we will not receive rewards for doing good but we will receive rewards for doing evil. If we have accepted God's only begotten son as our personal Savior and have lived for Him unto the end of our lives, we will not receive a reward or rewards for doing evil, but we will receive a reward for righteousness. It's time for us to be about not our own business but our father's business and our father's business is winning souls to Christ. We are saved by the grace of God to lead others to the grace of God. We are not working to be saved, but we are working with the Lord because we are saved. Jesus said in <u>John 9:4</u>, "I must work the works of Him that sent me, while it is day; the night cometh when no man can work". Jesus is letting us know here when He came into this world, He came to work. He did not come to be idle but He came to do the work of His heavenly father. Jesus said, I came down from

heaven not to do mine own will, but the will of Him that sent me. The Lord was sent by God into this world to seek and to save those who are lost. He said I must work the works of Him, my heavenly father that sent me. I must work while it is day. I must work while I am alive. The night cometh. In other words, the Lord was saying one day death which represents night, will come and no man will be able to work. We need to be found doing all that we can now while we can for the Lord, because just as sure as we are alive, one day we will die. After death, all of our working days will be over. We will then be called from labor to reward. Jesus also said in John 14:12, "Verily, verily, I say unto you, he that believth on me, the works that I do shall he do also, and greater works than these shall he do; because I go unto my Father". These were words of encouragement and expectation that Jesus gave to His disciples before He was crucified on the cross. Now the Lord is passing these same words to every believer all over this world. Jesus said those who believe in Him not those who do not believe in Him, would be able to do those works and even greater works than those that Jesus has done. Ten days after Jesus had ascended back to heaven, fifty days after His resurrection from the grave, when the day of Pentecost was fully come, the Lord sent the Holy Spirit to dwell in all believers' heart. The Holy Spirit is the one who empowers the believer to live for the Lord and do the works of God. Without the Holy Spirit, all of our working would be in vain. God speaks and works through the believer by His Holy Spirit. In order for the Holy Spirit to do the work of the Lord through us, we must submit ourselves to His authority. If you have not been filled with God's Holy Spirit, all you have to do is ask God to fill you. When we have been filled with the Holy Spirit and remain filled, there will be no room for evil to come into our heart. Time is running out. This world, in which we are living in, according to God's word, is fast approaching its end. Because of sin and demonic spirits, the love of many people has waxed cold. It's sad to say this, but even in many homes today, family love is gone. We are living in a day and time when it's time to go home, there are many family members from the husband and wife on down to the grandchildren who would rather go anywhere but home. This is so sad but God knows that it's true. The devil has been allowed to come into the family to kill, steal, and destroy. It's time for all those who do not know the Lord, get to know Him and then ask Him to help them take their love ones back. To all those who do not know the Lord, He is seated in heaven on the right hand of the Father, waiting on you to invite Him into your heart.

Revelation 3:20, "Behold, I stand at the door and knock, if any man hear my voice and open the door, I will come in to him, and will sup with him, and he with me". Jesus is saying to all those who do not know him, I am standing on the outside of the door to your heart knocking. I will not force my way into your heart. I will not knock the door down to your heart. If you hear my voice speaking to you, and will open the door of your heart, I will com in to you. I will come into your life now, not tomorrow, but now, I will come into your heart and live with you forever. Then when you come down to the last seconds of your life, I will be with you eternally. You will not have to worry about your soul because your soul will be with me forevermore. Amen.

CHAPTER NINE

What To Expect When We Get To Heaven

In heaven there will not be anymore tears. All of our crying days will be over because God Almighty shall wipe away all tears from our eyes. All over this world in which we live, people are crying because of things that have happened in their lives. But according to <u>Revelations 24:4</u>, our God has promised to wipe our eyes of all tears. In heaven, there <u>will not</u> be any more sorrow. In heaven, there <u>will not</u> be any more pain because all of the former things will pass away along with the first heaven and the first earth. God Almighty will make all things new. In heaven, there are twelve gates and also at the gates there are twelve angels. No one will be allowed to enter through those gates on their own terms, but they will enter through those gates only on God's terms. When I was coming up as a little boy in church, I use to hear some people say, "I'm going to heaven anyhow". It sounds to me like they were saying that they were going to heaven whether God like it or not. But I have found out now that the only way we will enter through one of those gates is that we MUST accept Jesus Christ as our personal Savior down here on earth before we die. We must be born again by the word of God and by the Spirit of God.

<u>Revelation 21:13</u> speaks about the separation of those twelve gates. On the east, there will be three gates; on the north, there will be three gates; on the south, there will be three gates and on the west there will be three gates. After the rapture of the church, Christians will enter into heaven and be brought in the presence of the Almighty God forever. These gates are not made of wood or iron, but of pearls. And

the streets are not streets of concrete or asphalt, neither will there be any potholes but Revelation 21:21 tells us that "the street of the city was pure gold, as it were transparent glass". In heaven, there will be no need of the sun neither of the moon to shine in it because the Glory of God will lighten the city and the Lamb Jesus, the son of God, is the light thereof. In heaven, the gates shall not be shut at all by day and there shall be no night there. Even though it is God's will that everyone go to heaven but because of wrong choices and decisions, many will not go to heaven. Revelation 21:27, "And there shall in no wise enter into it anything that defileth, neither whatsoever worketh abomination or maketh a lie: but they which are written in the Lamb's Book of Life". The only way that our name will be found in the book of life is that we must have accepted Jesus as our personal Savior and allow Him to live through us by His Holy Spirit. Again, my question to you is, "WHAT ABOUT YOUR SOUL?" Just as our physical body needs a place to rest after a long hard day of work, so does our soul needs an eternal place of rest and not an eternal place of suffering and torment. Heaven should be our goal each and every day of our lives. We should live everyday of our lives as though it was our last because we never know, it just might be. We must never take God's goodness and mercy for granted. Everyday that the Lord allows us to wake up and get up, we ought to get up with a made up mind to run for Jesus all that day. If we stumble and fall during that day, if we sin during that day, we should confess up to God, get up and get back into the race. Run for Jesus all the way unto the end until we hear God say "Well done, thou good and faithful servant". Then we know that our soul will rest eternally with the Lord. Revelation 14:13 The Lord told John to "Write, blesses are the dead which die in the Lord from henceforth: Yea, saith the spirit, that they may rest from their labours; and their works do follow them". One of these days, when this life down here is over, thanks be to God, we will be caught up in the rapture and our soul will be at rest with God. We will rest eternally from all those hours, days, months, and years of labor. Many times, we labored and people showed no appreciation. Many times we labored when we were physically burned out but because of the love for God in our heart, we pressed on anyhow. We labor for the Lord even when people talk about us and our work. We keep on laboring for the Lord when people misunderstand us; still we go on for the Lord anyhow, believing that our labor is not in vain. To keep on keeping on for the Lord, when the going gets tough, we must be fully persuaded that our God, whom we serve, is able to see us through no matter what we come up against. Our soul must be fully anchored in Jesus. When we are anchored in Jesus, it no longer matters about the storms. It no longer matters about the rain, when our soul is anchored in Jesus. It no longer matters about the floods because God will give us divine power to overcome and come out more than conquerors every time.

When you and I get to heaven, we can expect to meet Jesus face to face. We can expect to meet nobody but over comers, those who never gave up on God and themselves. They came out of great trials and great tribulations. In heaven, we will meet those who had many afflictions during their Christian walk with the Lord, but the Lord delivered them out of them all. Trouble will be no more. When you and I get to heaven, expect to see those that walked upright and spoke the truth in their heart. Jesus said none but the pure in heart shall see God. In heaven, expect to see those who did not backbite with their tongue, nor did they practice doing evil to their fellowman. 1 Corinthians 2:9, "But as it is written, eye hath not seen, nor ear heard, neither have entered into the heart of man, the things which God hath prepared for them that love Him". Verse 10, "But God hath revealed them unto us by His Spirit: for the spirit searcheth all things yea, the deep things of God". When all of God's children in Christ, come together, what a great time it will be!

CHAPTER TEN

What Not To Expect When We Get To Heaven

As a born again Christian, I cannot help but have great care and concern about everyone's soul. It's God's will and my desire as well, that all souls be saved. In this chapter it is not my intention to try to put anyone in hell or the lake of fire because I'm trying with all my heart, soul, mind, and strength to keep myself out. And if it wasn't for the Lord, I would fail in this big time. The Lord has said, Heaven and earth shall pass away but my words shall not pass away. So if the Lord has said it in His word, then these things must be. I am only writing about the things that the Lord has said will not be taking place in heaven. I am not rejoicing about these things but it's my prayer that these people will do like I did along with many others and that is confess their sins and ask the Lord to help them to turn from their sins. Then they too will experience God's love and forgiveness. Psalm 101:7 talks about the liar. It says, "He that telleth lies shall not tarry in my sight". Lies are from our adversary, the devil, because the devil is the father of all lies. In the eyesight of God, there is no such thing as a little lie or a big lie. They are all lies. The devil told the first lie when he spoke thought the serpent and told Eve, "Ye shall not surely die". When the Lord had already told the man on the day that thou eatest thereof o the tree of knowledge of good and evil, thou shalt surely die. This is the reason why a unrepented liar shall not tarry in God's sight. The devil used the serpent in the garden, but in our day and time, he is using people. God hates the lying but at the same time God still loves the liar. Many times when pressure is put on a person, if they don't watch themselves, they will do just what Peter did, one of the Lord's chosen disciples, when pressure was put on him. When pressure was put on Peter, he lied about his dealing with Jesus. Mark 14:71, "But he began to curse and to swear, saying, I know not this man of whom ye speak". Peter lied, still Jesus forgave him because when Mary Magdalene and the other women saw a young man at the grave, after Jesus was risen, he told them in Mark 16:7, "But go your way, tell his disciples and Peter that he goeth before you into Galilee". Even though Peter had lied and denied Jesus, the Lord still include Peter showing that even though Peter did lie more than one time, the Lord still loved Peter. This lets us know that the Lord still loves the liar but he hates the lying. There is a strong possibility that we all have told a lie or lies at one time or another. When we confessed to God, he forgave us of this sin and cleansed us from all unrighteousness. Since God has forgiven us, we ought to be willing to forgive others when they lie on us.

We must not expect to see false prophets in heaven. Jesus warned us about them in Matthew 7:15, "Beware of false prophets, which come to you in sheep's clothing, but inwardly they are ravening wolves". When a hungry, wild wolf come in contact with a harmless sheep, he has only one thing in mind and that is to have that sheep for his meal. Jesus is saying the same thing is true about a false prophet. They are just what they sound like, they are false. They are not real; they are not truthful. They will act like they are real. The will talk like they are real. They will walk like they are real. They will dress like they are real. They will try to even preach and teach like they are real. When they show up, they will have only one thing in mind and that will be to get all they can out of their prey and then move on to the next one. But when we walk with God, in time God will undress them and everyone will be able to see them for what they really are and that is a big fake! Jesus said in Matthew 7:16, "Ye shall know them by their fruits". What the Lord is saying here is that they can fake all they want to, but you will know them by the lifestyle they are living. There is one thing about a fake and that is time will reveal just what it is. The truth will always stand but a fake, that which is not real, in time will be brought down and undressed. In Matthew 7:21-23, the Lord is letting us know what not to expect when we get to heaven, when it comes down to certain people in the church. Verse 21 clearly lets us know that calling on the name of the Lord will not be enough when the heart and motives are not real. "Not everyone that saith unto me, Lord, Lord, shall enter into the kingdom of heaven; but he that doeth the will of my father which is in heaven". This verse clearly lets us know that just by saying the name of Jesus, will not be enough for us to make it to heaven. But the Lord is letting us know that after we have heard the word of God, we must then receive the word and then become a doer of the word. Because doing what the word of God tells us to do is what's going to cause us to enter the kingdom of heaven. Obedience to the word of God is what gets God's attention. God is not just looking for someone who will just talk the word but our God is looking for someone who will allow Him to put His word in their heart. When God's word is in our heart, then and only then are we able to do the will of God. Because it is no longer us doing it, but it is God. When Jesus was led up of the spirit into the wilderness to be tempted of the devil, Jesus told the devil in Matthew 4:4, "It is written, man shall not live by bread alone, but by every word that proceedeth out of the mouth of God". As we live by the word of God daily, this is what will cause us to make it into God's kingdom. Verse 22, "Many will say to me in that day, Lord, Lord, have we not prophesied in thy name? and in thy name have cast out devils? And in thy name done many wonderful works?" On the day of judgment, there will be church goers standing in the presence of the Lord trying to remind the Lord of the things they have done. But all the while they were doing these things, they did not know the Lord. They did not have a personal relationship with the Lord. They knew of the Lord through someone else's experience, but they did not know the Lord for themselves. There were convinced that their works were good enough to save them and cause them to go to heaven. Wonderful works won't save us but accepting Jesus as our personal Savior will. This is what qualifies us to do the work of the Lord. The worst thing that we can do in our life is to live in this world for years and die, then stand in the judgment expecting to live eternally with the Lord only to hear Him say I don't know you. Verse 23, "And then will I profess unto them, I never knew you: depart from me ye that work iniquity". If the Lord says I never knew you, we will be in eternal trouble. So now is the time to accept the Lord on this side of life before we die. Because after death then comes the judgment. In these verses, these people did not know Jesus and because they did not know Jesus, when they stood before the Lord on that great day, the Lord did not know them. Not only did the Lord not know them, but He also told them to get away from me. I don't know about you, but I don't want the Lord to say this to me. What I want the Lord to say to me is what He said in <u>Matthew 25:21</u>, "Well done, thou good and faithful servant: thou hast been faithful over a few things, I will make thee ruler over many things: enter thou into the joy of thy Lord". The joy that we experience in this world is short lived but when we get to heaven, the Lord's joy will have no end. When the Lord comes back, He will come in His glory and all His holy angels with Him. And before Him shall be gathered all nations and He shall separate them one from another, as a shepherd divideth his sheep from the goats, <u>Matthew 25:31-32</u>. When the lord comes again, He will separate the right from the wrong. When the Lord comes back, he will separate the righteous from the wicked.

CHAPTER ELEVEN

Paying The Price For Following God

The price for salvation has already been paid in full by the precious blood of Jesus. But following God is a daily price that every Christian must pay down here on earth if they expect to live eternally with God. Mountains will be high, and valleys will be low as we pay the price for following God. Friends will become few and enemies will become many as we pay the price for following God. Following God will not be a cake walk, that's why Paul told Timothy in 2 Timothy 2:3, "Thou therefore endure hardness as a good soldier of Jesus Christ". Paul is letting Timothy know here that the road will be rough and the going will get tough as he follows God. The same will be true for us also. Psalm 34:19 tells us "Many are the afflictions of the righteous: but the Lord deivereth him out of them all". In other words, what David is saying to us is, if God be for us, who can be against us. When God is for us, no weapon that is formed against us shall prosper. When God is for us, enemies can be all around us, still they will not be able to stop God from taking good care of us. That's why David said in Psalm 23:5, "Thou prepares a table before me in the presence of mine enemies". When our ways please the Lord, He will make our enemies to be at peace with us. What a mighty God we serve. As we pay the price for following God, there will be some people that we will not be able to run with because they will hinder our walk with God. A good example of this is what the Lord told Abram to do. Genesis 12:1, "Now the Lord had said to Abram, get thee out of thy country, and from thy kindred, and from thy father's house, unto a land that I will shew thee". In the eyesight of God, Abram was in the wrong place. Abram was around the wrong people. Many times being around the wrong people who do not believe as we believer will cause us to remain infants Christians. We will not receive the fullness of God's blessings. Abram would not receive the great blessings of God until he removed himself out of the environment that he was use to living in. The Lord told Abram, if you move out by faith, I will bless you. I will make of thee a great nation and I will bless thee and make thy name great: and thou shalt be a blessing. Not only is there a cross to bear down here for the Lord, but there are many blessings to be received also as we pay the price for following God. God did just what He promised Abram that He would do. Genesis 13:2, "And Abram was very rich in cattle, in silver, and in gold". Again, our God is a keeper of His word. If God has said it, He will do it. If God has spoken it, He will make it good.

Shadrach, Meshach, and Abednego paid the price for following God when they refused to bow and worship the gold image that the king had set up. Because they refused to bow, they were given the death penalty, which was a burning, fiery furnace heated seven times hotter than it was suppose to be. When we have a made up mind to follow God, our adversary the devil will turn the heat up on us also to try to get our focus off of God. When we stand still our God will come through and fight our battle for us every time. Before these three were thrown in the fiery furnace, they stood unified and fully persuaded about the power of their God. They told the king in Daniel 3:17, "If it be so, our God whom we serve is able to deliver us from the burning fiery furnace, and He will deliver us out of thine hand O king". They went on to tell him in Verse 18, "But if not, be it known unto thee, O king, that we will not serve they gods, nor worship the golden image which house hast set up". Theses believers had made up minds that they were going to serve and worship the Almighty God only and even if God did not come through for them as they expected, they were willing to lay down their lives for the God that they believed in. When we trust in the Lord with all our heart, God will never leave us nor will He forsake us. When these believers stood up for the God they believed in, the Lord came into the midst and stood with them and delivered them. Daniel 3:23-25, "And these three men, Shadrach, Meshach, and Abednego fell down bound into the midst of the burning fiery furnace". Verse 24, "Then Nebuchadnezzar the king was astonished, and rose up in haste, and spake and said unto his counsellors, Did not we cast three men bound into the midst of the fire? They answered and said unto the king, True, O king". <u>Verse 25</u>, "He answered and said, Lo, I see four men loose, walking in the midst of the fire, and they have no hurt: and the form of the fourth is like the son of God". If we get into trouble for following the will of the Lord, then God is obligated to get us out of it. When these men were thrown into the fire, the Lord went into the fire with them. No only did the Lord go into the fire with them, but while in the fire, the Lord took total control of the fire and brought them out of the fire harmless. <u>Verse 27</u>, "And the princes, governors, and captains, and the kings counsellors, being gathered together, saw these men upon whose bodies the fire had no power, nor was an hair of their head singed neither were their coats changed, nor the smell of fire had passed on them". Because these three men were willing to pay the price for following God, the Lord stepped in and took the power from the fire. The Lord was a shield of protection for these men. He kept them from all hurt, all harm, and all danger. If the Lord did this for them, he will do it also for us if we are willing to pay the price for following God. You may be in a fiery situation now as you read this book but I want to put you in remembrance of what these men said, Our God whom we serve is able, and He will deliver us out of whatever our adversary the devil puts us in. Our God is greater than all.

Joseph was willing to pay the price for following God. Joseph dreamed a dream and told it to his brethren: and they hated him yet the more <u>Genesis 37:5</u>. There are some people, many times in our family, who don't want to dream and don't want anyone else to dream. Because of this, we must be very careful who we share our God given dreams with. Because the devil has people out there that he will use against us and these people are called dream killers. They will come into our lives with a one track mind and that is to kill the God given dream that the Lord has given to us. Joseph's own brothers did all they could in their power to kill their brothers dream. So they figured it out! To kill the dream, they needed to kill the dreamer. They finally ended up selling their own brother as a salve and he was taken down to Egypt. While down in Egypt, Joseph was still willing to pay the price for following God. Because of this, the Lord was with Joseph in all that he did. <u>Genesis 39:2-3</u>, "And the Lord was with Joseph, and he was a prosperous man; and he was in the house of his master the Egyptian.

And his master saw that he Lord was with him, and that the Lord made all that he did to prosper in his hand". Even while serving as a slave under another man's roof, the Lord caused everything that Joseph did to prosper. The Lord was working so mightily in Joseph's life until his master, a man who no doubt did not know Joseph's God, was able to see God at work in Joseph's life. No matter what the situation may be that we find ourselves in, those who don't know God should be inspired to get to know Him because they see Him living in our lives. As we suffer according to the will of God, God will give us power to overcome and come out of the situation more than conquers. Because God was with Joseph, he was promoted to overseer of the Egyptian's whole household, all because Joseph was willing to pay the price for following God.

Paul and Silas, two men of God, were also willing to pay the price for following God. Acts 16:22-26, Verse 22, "And the multitude rose up together against them: and the magistrates rent off their clothes, and commanded to beat them". Here we have Paul and Silas suffering because of the will of God. A whole city has come against them but this still will not stop God from making a way out of no way. These men's clothes were torn off of them. All that is exposed now is their flesh. The order has been given by upper authorities to beat Paul and Silas. Verse 23, "And when they had laid many stripes upon them, they cast them into prison, charging the jailor to keep them safe". After Paul and Silas had been beaten, they were not released but they were thrown into prison. Then pressure was put on the jailer, the one in charge for locking prisoners up and keeping them locked up. The jailer's life would be taken if Paul or Silas were to escape. So the jailer knew that he had to do all within his power to not let these men escape. So he put them in an area of the prison where he knew they would not be able to escape. Verse 24, "Who, having received such a charge, thrust them into the inner prison and made their feet fast in the stocks". The keeper of the prison threw Paul and Silas into the maximum security area of the prison which was the inner prison. Then before he left out of the cell where these men of God were, he put stocks, ankle lock, around these men's ankles so that if they did escape out of the prison cell, they still would not be able to run. So here we have Paul and Silas not only locked up in prison but they are also locked down. No doubt they are bleeding and their bodies are racking with pain and their movements are limited. Instead of Paul and Silas focusing on the circumstances that they are in, they began to look beyond these circumstances and focused on their God. The one that they knew was able to make a way out of no way. They were not sitting in the prison cell complaining. They did not blame God for the condition that they found themselves in. Neither did they blame one another. What these two men of God did was they began to look unto the hills from whence cometh their help. These men knew that their help came from the Lord, the one who created heaven and earth. Verse 25, "And at midnight Paul and Silas prayed, and sang praises unto God and the prisoners heard them". At midnight, the ending of one day; at midnight, the beginning of another day. Not just one prayed, neither did just one sing. But at midnight, both men, Paul and Silas, began to lift up the mighty name of Jesus. The Lord has said, If I be lifted up from the earth, I will draw all men unto me. It has also been said, when praises go up, blessing will come down. Praising God with a real pure heart will bring God on the scene. Paul and Silas were not ashamed of their God because as they prayed and sang praises to God, the prisoners heard them. In other words, more than one person heard these men. Not only did the prisoners hear them in the cell next to them, but it's possible that these men of God could have been heard three cells down, six cells down, ten or fifteen cells down. Paul and Silas prayed and sang to the Almighty God. Who is still a way out of no way. If there is no way out then our God will create a way out. Verse 26, "And suddenly there was a great earthquake, so that the foundations of the prison were shaken: and immediately all the doors were opened, and every one's bands were loosed". Again, what we see here is our Almighty God making a way where there was no way. Not only did God hear Paul and Silas' prayer and praise, but God answered their prayer by sending a great earthquake. We also see God working in this earthquake because it did not shake the roof or upper part of the prison but God caused the earthquake to shake the bottom of the prison. When this happened, right then and there, not just the door where Paul and Silas were opened, but all the doors of the prison were opened. Maximum security could not stop God. Then everyone's bands were loosed. Even the prisoners who did not know God were loosed. The prisoners who did not join in and pray with Paul and Silas were loosed. Even the prisoners who did not sing praises to God with Paul and Silas were loosed. What we see happening in this prison is God being good to the just and the unjust. Because Paul and Silas were willing to pay the price for following God, when they called on God, He came quickly to their rescue. Also, the keeper of the prison and his house were all saved. The keeper of the prison and his family accepted the Lord as their personal Savior. Verse 30-31, "And brought them out, and said, Sirs, what must I do to be saved? And they said, believe on the Lord Jesus Christ, and thou shalt be saved, and thy house". Because of Paul and Silas, God was glorified by their lifestyle that they lived before these prisoners and the keeper of the prison and his family souls would live eternally with God. What about your soul? Again, please don't do what many have already done and that's put off until it was too late. If anyone dies before accepting Jesus as their personal Savior, it will be too late. Because after death comes the judgment.

As I close this book, Jesus, the son of God, came into this world and paid the price for following God. Jesus told his disciples one day I came down from heaven not to do my will, but the will of Him that sent me. Jesus was sent by His heavenly Father into this world to die for the sins of the world. Jesus came to die for sinners not saints.

John 3:16, "For God so loved the world that He gave His only begotten son, that whosoever believeth in Him should not perish but have everlasting life". Whoever accepts Jesus as their personal Savior, their soul will not live eternally in the lake of fire. What should be admired about our God here is that He gave all that He had and He gave the best that He had. When God gave Jesus, God gave Himself. No one else was worthy to pay the price for man's sin but God's only begotten son. One day Jesus and His disciples went to the mount of Olives after arriving there He encouraged them to do what He Himself was about to do and that was pray to His heavenly Father, Luke 22:41-44. Verse 41, "And He was withdrawn from them about a stone's cast, and kneeled down, and prayed". If Jesus had to pray to keep on keeping on, what about you and me? It's God's will that men pray always and not faint. Everyday of our lives, we need to get away from everybody and go down on our knees and pray to God our Father. Sincere prayer will keep us pressing on with God. Sincere prayer will keep us strong in the Lord and in the power of His might. When was the last time that you prayed to God Almighty? Verse 42, "Saying, Father, If thou be willing, remove this cup from me: nevertheless no my will, but thine, be done". As Jesus prayed to His heavenly Father, He was focused toward Calvary and the sinful death that He was about to die. Also, in this prayer there is a struggle between the flesh and the spirit. The flesh, the physical man, is asking God to remove the cup of suffering from Jesus. Then we have the spiritual man, the Spirit of God, being obedient to God, and the will of God. Jesus said on one occasion, the Spirit is will but the flesh is weak.

Our prayers will be more sincere to God because we are totally depending on God to answer our prayer. As Jesus prayed, his physical body was reacting to what it was about to go through on Calvary. As we walk with God, many times if it wasn't for the Lord helping us, we would not be able to endure some of the things that we <u>must go through</u>. As we follow the Lord, we too will suffer many things at the hands of sinful me n and saved men. <u>Luke 23:33</u>, We see the will of God being fulfilled though His only begotten son. "And when they were come to the place, which is called Calvary, there they crucified Him and the malefactors, one on the right hand and the other on the left". Jesus is paying the price which no one was worthy to pay but Him. He gave His life, a dying sacrifice, so that we would accept Him as our personal Savior and live our lives a living sacrifice for Him. Here we have the son of God between two criminals. A righteous God dying along with two worldly men. But what's good about this is, Jesus is not dead! He is alive and alive forevermore! <u>Luke 23:53</u>, "And He took it down, and wrapped it in linen, and laid it in a sepulcher that was hewn in stone, wherein never man before was laid". After Jesus died on the cross, there was a man by the name of Joseph, a counsellor, a good man and a just man. Joseph went to Pilate and begged for the body of Jesus. After Pilate, the Roman governor, gave him permission, Joseph went and took the body of Jesus down and wrapped it in linen. Then after wrapping the body of Jesus in linen, he laid it in a walk in grave cut in stone. This was a brand new grave because no man had been laid there before. Jesus died and He was buried but that's not the end because He got up! <u>Luke 24:2-3</u>, "And they found the stone rolled away from the sepulcher. And they entered in and found not the body of the Lord Jesus". The next day very early in the morning came Mary Magdalene and Mary the mother of James with spices to anoint the body of Jesus. But when they got there they found out that they were too late, even though it was very early in the morning. Also they would not be able to use the spices on the body of Jesus which is good news for all those who will believe and accept God's plan for salvation. <u>Verse 3</u>, "And they entered in, and found not the body of the Lord Jesus". As these women went into the tomb, they found out that the Lord was already gone because there was no body to be anointed with the spices. As they stood there confused, two men stood by them in shinning garments. In other words, two God sent angels brought them some comforting words. These angels had a question for these women and that question was, why seek ye the living among the dead. This lets us know the Lord is not the God of the dead but of the living. These angels were letting these women know they were looking for Jesus in the wrong place. The same thing is true about many people today. And that is they are looking for Jesus in the wrong places. Jesus will not be found among the dead, but the living. These women were told Jesus was not there but is risen. Then they reminded these women of what Jesus had said when He was yet alive; when He was still in Galilee. Jesus said, "The Son of Man must be delivered into the hands of sinful men and be crucified, and the third day rise again". The Lord did exactly what He said He would do. The third day He got up and walked out of the grave. Acts 1:8-11 we see the promise of divine power and the Lord returning back to heaven. Verse 8, "But ye shall receive power, after that the Holy Ghost is come upon you: and ye shall be witnesses unto me both in Jerusalem and in all Judaea, and in Samaria and unto the uttermost part of the earth". On the day of Pentecost, the Holy Ghost came in as a rushing might wind. And they, the believers who were all on one accord and in one place, were all filled with the Holy Ghost and began to speak with other tongues as the Spirit gave them utterance. Every since the day of Pentecost, God has been filling believers with the Holy Ghost. Have you been filled with the Holy Ghost? Verse 9, "And when he had spoken these things, while they beheld, he was taken up; and a cloud received him out of their sight". After Jesus spoke these words of promise to His disciples, He ascended back up into heaven from whence He came. Verse 10, "And while they looked steadfastly toward heaven as He went up, behold, two men stood by them in white apparel". Verse 11, "Which also said, ye men of Galilee, why stand ye gazing up into heaven? This same Jesus which is taken up from you into heaven, shall so come in like manner as ye have seen Him go into heaven". As Jesus' disciples stood there looking at the Lord as He was taken up, again, two angels had a question for them. Why are you standing here looking up into heaven? This same Jesus is coming back the same way that you saw Him go up into heaven. If the Lord would come back in this very hour as you are reading this book, will your soul spend eternity with God or eternally separated from God? No one can answer this question but you. Just as we prepare to live in this world, we must also prepare to leave out of this world.

Jesus will come back at a time when many will not be prepared for His coming. When the Lord comes back there will be a great payday for the whole human race. Revelation 22:12, "And, behold, I come quickly and my reward with me, to give every man according as his works shall be". We know not the day nor hour that the Lord will return. He did not tell us to get ready but he told us to be ready. The only way that we can be ready is that we must accept Jesus Christ as our person Savior. When the Lord comes back, He will pay me according to the works that I have done in my body, whether they were good works or evil works. When the Lord comes back, he will pay you according to all the works that you have done in your body, whether they be good or whether they be bad. Don't be deceived by those who do not believe because Jesus has said, "Surely I come quickly Revelation 22:20.

After we have all been judged, then our eternal soul will spend eternity in one of two places, with God in heaven or separated from God in the lake of fire. I don't know about you, but I can always speak for myself, I have made up my mind that I'm going to pay the price for following God on this side of life. Because I don't' want my soul to be separated from God forever and I know you don't want this either. So if you have not done this yet, do it now before you die. Accept Jesus as your personal Savior now! Then your soul will have a place of eternal rest, eternal peace, eternal joy, eternal happiness with God the Father, God the Son, and the Holy Spirit forever.

What about your soul? As we come to the close of this book, the Lord told me to leave this with you, about the questions that He asked in Matthew 16:26, "For what is a man profited, if he shall gain the whole world, and lose his own soul? Or what shall a man give in exchange for his soul?" Our Lord and Savior Jesus Christ is asking the most important questions that could ever be asked and they are dealing with the eternal soul of man. Jesus is asking the question, what will man get out of this if he gains all the material wealth that this world has to offer, then after he dies and stand before God, because he took no time out for God, he did not accept Jesus Christ as his personal

Savior, so he died as a unbeliever. Because of this his soul will be lost, lost to eternal separation from God. Lost to the second death which is the death of the lake of fire. In other words, if a person ends up dying separated from the Lord, all of their work and labor will all be in vain. When we stand before God in the judgment, material things will not be able to help us. In the judgment, we will not be able to bargain or make a deal with God because the earth is the Lord's and the fulness thereof; the world and they that dwell therein. So we cannot give to God what already belongs to God. There will be no exchange, only knowing and living for Jesus while we were alive here on earth will enable us to live eternally with God. The Lord has promised when He comes, He shall reward every man according to his works. So the number one work that we should be doing while it is day, while we are alive, is the work of the Lord. Jesus said in Matthew 20:4, "Go ye also into the vineyard, and whatsoever is right I will give you". The vineyard represents the world. You and I are saved to encourage others to be saved. Jesus again said for us, the church, to let your light so shine before men that they may see your good work and glorify your Father which is in heaven. The Lord has told the believer ye are the light of the world, a city that sits on a hill cannot be hid. As we humble ourselves, deny ourselves, and take up our cross daily and follow Jesus, God will be glorified through us and cause others to be drawn to Him.

WHAT ABOUT YOUR SOUL?

Notes

Notes

About the Author

I am a born again Christian who accepted the Lord as my personal Savior in the year of 1975. I accepted my call into the gospel ministry on November 12, 1989. I was called to Pastor some of God's sheep in March of 1993. I presently sever as Pastor of the St. John Missionary Baptist Church of Bossier City, LA. I discovered my gift as a writer in 2000. When I write, there is a God given peace upon me, assuring me that I am fulfilling one of God's purposes for me being here.

For more information on this book, you may contact:
Pastor Johnny James
St John Missionary Baptist Church
1701 E. Texas Street
Bossier City, LA 71111
Church Ph (318) 742-8778
Other (318) 820-4546
Email: pastorjjames@hotmail.com